SYSTEMS OF GOVERNMENT

DICTATORSHIP

Paul Dowswell

Evans

Published by Evans Brothers Limited
2A Portman Mansions
Chiltern Street
London W1U 6NR

Planned and produced for Evans Brothers by Book Factory Limited.

First published 2005
© copyright Evans Brothers 2005

Dowswell, Paul
Dictatorship. - (Systems of government)
1. Dictatorship - Juvenile literature
2. Dictatorship - History - Juvenile literature
I. Title
321'9

Published and bound by A.G.G. Printing Stars

ISBN 0237527006

Editor: Patience Coster
Designer: Jane Hawkins
Illustrations: Stefan Chabluk
Consultant: Michael Rawcliffe
We are grateful to the following for permission to reproduce photographs: Ali Jarekji/Reuters/Corbis 37; Andre Kaiser/Rex/SIPA 41; Araldo de Luca/Corbis 4; Bernard Bisson/Corbis Sygma 8; Bettmann/Corbis 7, 15, 17; Corbis 26; Hulton-Deutsch Collection/Corbis 14, *front cover* and 21; Keystone/Rex *front cover*; Keystone/The Image Works/Topham 5; Lehtikuva/Rex 36; Les Stone/Corbis 9; Novosti/Topham 16, 19; Pablo Corral V/Corbis 10; Reuters/Corbis 38, 43; Rex/SIPA 13, 34, 40, 42; Roger Viollet/Rex 22; Topfoto 35; Topham/Ann Ronan/Hip 27; Topham/Associated Press 23, 28, 30, 33; Topham Picturepoint 12, 18, 25, *title page* and 32.

In this book, dates are written using BCE and CE, instead of BC and AD which are based on the Christian calendar. BCE means 'Before the Common Era' and it replaces BC (Before Christ). CE means 'in the Common Era' and it replaces AD ('Anno Domini – in the year of our Lord').

CONTENTS

CHAPTER 1

What is Dictatorship?

In 1887, the British historian Lord Acton made the connection between power and corruption (immorality). He said: 'Power tends to corrupt, and absolute power corrupts absolutely.' A look at the history of dictatorship – the unbridled rule of one person who imposes his or her will on the government of a country – shows that these words are all too true. The twentieth century in particular saw large parts of the world in the grip of various dictatorships, and almost every one of them left a trail of human destruction and misery in its wake. The most notable dictators of the century, Germany's Adolf Hitler, Russia's Joseph Stalin and China's Mao Zedong, were responsible for the deaths of millions of people, and presided over three of the most inhuman regimes in history. They also inflicted their system of government on other nations they had brought under their rule by armed conquest. Lesser dictators, such as Argentina's General Leopoldo Galtieri, and Italy's Benito Mussolini, brought division, repression and war to their nations too. Fortunately, the damage they caused was restricted because their countries were not so powerful.

Julius Caesar, one of ancient history's most famous dictators. His attempt to seize absolute power in Rome ended in his murder.

Rule by absolute power

It is difficult to be precise about the meaning of the word 'dictatorship', because it has changed over time. In essence, it is a system of government where one person – a dictator – has absolute power as leader of his or her country. This means there are no laws, or fellow government ministers, or political opponents to stop the dictator doing exactly what he or she wants to do.

Dictatorship is completely different from democracy, a system of government that has agreed guidelines describing how a country should be run. For example, in a democracy there is often a constitution or set of rules that states how a government should be allowed to govern. There is also the rule of law – which means that every citizen, regardless of wealth or class, is treated equally according to an agreed set of rules. In a democracy, people are expected to respect these rules,

> **Dictatorships do not grow out of strong and successful governments, but out of weak and helpless ones.**
>
> *US president, Franklin Delano Roosevelt, speaking in 1938.*

> **"Every activity and every need of every individual will be regulated... by the Party... there are no longer any free realms in which the individual belongs to himself. The time of personal happiness is over."**
>
> *In Mein Kampf (1924), a book in which he described his philosophy, Adolf Hitler outlines his plans for dictatorship by the Nazi Party in Germany.*

Common features

Dictators of whatever complexion have all or most of the following features in common:

- Many seize power by force – using their country's army, or their own private armies, or they cheat in elections to gain power.
- They intimidate the population, using the threat of arrest, torture and execution to hold on to power.
- They take away the civil liberties of their citizens – for example, they remove people's right to free speech and their right to oppose the government of their country.
- They use the media – newspapers, radio, posters, cinema, and more recently television and the Internet – relentlessly to press home their message. At the same time, they forbid the airing of any opposing views to their regime in the media.

Adolf Hitler, one of modern history's most infamous dictators. Hitler is shown here at a Nazi rally in Dortmund, Germany, in 1933.

which distinguish between acceptable behaviour and criminal behaviour. In a democracy, even the leaders (including presidents and prime ministers) must obey the law. In a dictatorship, no attention is paid either to a constitution or to the rule of law – dictators can make up their own rules, and break them, as they see fit.

Dictatorship is a system of government – but it is also a style of leadership. Dictatorships can occur under any political system in crisis. Dictators such as Hitler in Germany and Mussolini in Italy have controlled extreme, right-wing, fascist regimes. But dictators have also controlled extreme, left-wing, communist governments (for example, Stalin in Russia and Nicolae Ceauçescu in Romania). Dictators do not necessarily hold any one set of political beliefs, although most are from the far right or far left of the political spectrum. Sometimes elected leaders go on to suspend a democratic form of government and become dictators, as Hitler did in Germany.

Many countries have suffered dictatorships because of the influence of other more powerful nations. For example, before his overthrow in 2003, Saddam Hussein of Iraq was supported by Western nations because he was seen as a stabilising influence in his oil-rich nation and a staunch opponent of Muslim fundamentalism. During the Cold War, the USA and the Soviet Union supported a range of brutal dictators because they were important as allies.

The roots of dictatorship

Today, for most people, the word 'dictator' has an obviously negative meaning. Originally, however, the idea of dictatorship was seen as a positive one. The word itself comes from the republic of Ancient Rome (510–27 BCE), when a single leader with absolute authority was chosen to rule during a period of great crisis, such as an invasion or rebellion. These Roman dictators controlled their country for a limited period of no more than six months at a time. Their powers, although extensive, were still limited by agreed laws. More recent dictators, however, have borne a closer resemblance not to Roman rulers but to the tyrants of Ancient Greece (800–30 BCE). Like Pisistratus of Athens (c.600–527 BCE), these were usually ambitious military leaders who used their armies to seize control. These tyrants ignored existing laws and clung on to power ruthlessly. Often their rule only ended when they died or were killed.

Modern-day dictators

The first modern-day dictators emerged in the nineteenth and early twentieth centuries. They came to power in Europe and Latin America. Some of the countries over which they gained control had been ruled for centuries by traditional monarchies, where the law of heredity was observed. (This meant the ruler was always succeeded by his eldest son or daughter.) Others were former European colonies, which had recently gained their independence. These modern-day dictators can be described as authoritarian. This means they demanded strict obedience from their citizens and ruthlessly punished any opposition – but they did not attempt to control every aspect of people's lives.

In the first half of the twentieth century, a far more destructive type of dictator came to power. This was partly because of advances in communications, such as widespread access to radio and cinema. Broadcasts and newsreels enabled dictators to press home a particular message and allowed them to exert far greater control over their population than ever before. The twentieth-century leaders ruled over so-called 'totalitarian' regimes that had absolute control over every aspect of the lives of their citizens. Of these dictators, Hitler, Stalin, Mussolini, General Francisco Franco of Spain and Mao Zedong in China are probably the best known.

In this photo, Spain's General Franco mixes the classic dictatorship traits of power and spectacle as he reviews troops in Madrid in 1939.

During the Cold War period following the Second World War, a
rash of dictatorships appeared in Eastern Europe, Latin America,
Africa and Asia. Some of these sprang up when countries were
given their independence by the colonial powers (for example,
Britain, France and Holland) that had previously controlled them.
Others came about as the result of a revolution against another
form of repressive government. Some of the dictatorships that
arose were left-wing, others were right-wing. They were usually
supported by either one of the two post-war superpowers – with
the Soviet Union usually supporting left-wing dictatorships and
the USA usually supporting right-wing ones. Other dictatorships,
especially those in Eastern Europe, were set up by the Soviet
Union in territory it had overrun during the Second World War.
Since the end of the Cold War and the collapse of the Soviet
Union in 1989, democratic governments have gradually replaced
many of these dictatorships.

There are still dictators in the world today, especially in
Africa, Asia and the Middle East. But dictatorship as a form of
government is becoming less common, and it is more difficult for
dictators to hold on to their power now that there is only one
superpower (the USA) left in the world. During the Cold War era,
the rival powers relied on dictators to support their interests, and
most of these dictators needed propping up by the superpowers
in order to survive. Recent events in Afghanistan and Iraq have
seen the overthrow of totalitarian regimes as a result of direct
armed intervention by the USA. It remains to be seen whether
these interventions by a foreign power will lead to a change from
dictatorship to democracy.

*The Romanian dictator Nicolae
Ceauçescu attends to government
business in November 1989. By the
end of the year he would be dead –
executed following a popular uprising
against his corrupt rule.*

Why dictatorships arise

From ancient times onwards, dictatorship has usually been a response to a desperate situation. This may be the threat of civil war, the collapse of the economy, the danger of invasion, or the need to depose a corrupt and incompetent leader and restore order and confidence. This form of government is not characteristic of a stable, prosperous, contented society.

Yet even staunch democracies resort to some of the characteristics of dictatorship in times of crisis, granting 'emergency powers' outside the constitution or rule of law to the president or prime minister or to a small inner circle of government colleagues. The exercising of these emergency powers may involve censoring the media or removing certain civil rights. Such moments are fraught with danger. After all, Hitler and Mussolini both seized control by extending the use of emergency powers into a prolonged dictatorship. In the USA and UK, the restrictions brought about by the granting of such emergency powers during wartime (for example, during the Second World War) ended when the war was over. In these instances, the US and UK governments had a long tradition of democracy, and both countries were relatively prosperous and were victors in the war. In less favourable circumstances, perhaps they too might have succumbed to dictatorship?

> **Those republics which in time of danger cannot resort to a dictator will generally be ruined when grave occasions occur.**
>
> Renaissance political commentator Nicoli Machiavelli (1469–1527).

In the streets of Addis Ababa in 1991 rebel forces burn a portrait of Ethiopian dictator Haile Mariam Mengistu during a successful uprising against him.

CHAPTER 2

Authoritarian Dictators

The first dictators of modern times can be found in nineteenth-century Latin America and early twentieth-century Europe. These leaders rose to power when traditional styles of government, such as monarchy or colonial rule, had resulted in countries run by weak, corrupt or exploitative administrations.

> **He who serves the revolution ploughs the sea.**

A popular saying in Latin American politics which affirms the belief that all revolutions are bound to fail in their good intentions, much as ploughing the sea is an impossible task.

This equestrian statue of Símon Bolívar can be found in the Plaza Bolívar in Caracas, Venezuela.

In Latin America during the early nineteenth century, countries struggled to gain independence from European colonial powers such as Spain and Portugal. When these countries withdrew, effective government collapsed. Men such as Símon Bolívar in Venezuela, Colombia and Peru, Santa Anna in Mexico, and Juan Manuel de Rosas in Argentina rose up to fill the power vacuum that had resulted from this collapse.

The liberator of Latin America

A Venezuelan aristocrat, Símon Bolívar led several Latin American countries to independence against Spanish colonial rulers who, between the sixteenth and the nineteenth centuries, controlled most of the continent. Bolívar drove the Spanish out of Colombia in 1819 and from Venezuela in 1821, and he went on to lead an army into Peru that same year to defeat Spanish forces there. In 1822, Bolívar liberated Ecuador and then, in 1825, an area known as Upper Peru, which was renamed Bolivia in his honour.

During these wars of liberation, other local leaders rebelling against colonial rule offered Bolívar the presidency of Gran Columbia – a territory that now comprises Venezuela, Colombia, Ecuador and Panama. Bolívar's dream was to unite the whole of Spanish-speaking Latin America in a similar form to the different states in the United States of America. Not everyone liked the idea, and the confederation of Gran Columbia did not last. Bolívar believed that strong, central government was the only way to unite these countries, which were divided by regional and racial differences and where rivalry between the capital and the provinces, and government and military, was a constant source of friction. Suffering from tuberculosis, and unpopular because he was considered to be a dictator, Bolívar resigned in 1830. He died in December of that year. At the time of his death, Bolívar was so disliked that his home country, Venezuela, refused to allow his body to be buried there. But history has viewed him in a kinder light. Today in Latin America he is regarded as a hero because of his pivotal role in liberating the continent from domination by European colonial powers.

Crises in Latin America

Like most former colonies, the newly liberated nations of Latin America found it difficult adjusting to life without the strong central government that had ruled them from Spain. Although they were rich in natural resources, their populations were poorly educated and there was little sense of national unity. By the 1820s a pattern had emerged whereby these countries began to fall under the control of local *caudillos* (strong men). This form of leadership was a direct response to the need for firm government in time of crisis. The *caudillos* were usually rich landowners who recruited private armies – usually from peasants who worked on their estates. Sometimes the *caudillos* controlled their own region, sometimes they took control of the entire country.

This modern map of Latin American countries shows the areas that were once controlled by Spain and Portugal.

Conquistadors

Latin America was colonised by Spain and Portugal following voyages of exploration by Christopher Columbus between 1492 and 1504. By the end of the sixteenth century, the continent had fallen under the control of these countries largely as a result of the superior fighting skills and weapons of the Spanish and Portuguese conquistadors (conquerors). The Portuguese, who had first settled along its coast, controlled Brazil. Spain held the rest of the continent. Both these European powers established strong colonial governments and imposed their cultures on the existing Latin American populations. But by the early nineteenth century both Spain and Portugal were in decline and no longer able to impose their will upon the Latin American colonies.

Areas occupied by the Spanish at the end of the 16th century

Areas occupied by the Portuguese at the end of the 16th century

11

Juan Manuel de Rosas was one such *caudillo*, who seized power in Argentina in 1835. He ruled with great brutality, persecuting his political enemies and forbidding any open opposition to his rule. But de Rosas was also able to unite his new country and defend it from the attentions of two strong colonial powers, Britain and France. He was eventually overthrown by another *caudillo* in 1853.

Paraguay had a more unfortunate experience of rule by *caudillo*. Francisco Solano López was a dictator who greatly admired the French emperor, Napoleon III, who had seized power in France in 1848. (Napoleon had declared himself emperor and attempted to modernise France by building up its territory and invading other nations.) Between 1865 and 1870, in an attempt to create a Paraguayan empire at the heart of the continent, López waged war against Brazil, Uruguay and Argentina. The war only ended when he was killed in battle.

Unfortunately for Paraguay, López's ambitions far exceeded the capabilities of his country. Half the population of Paraguay was killed in the war, which also devastated the country's economy and brought agriculture to a standstill. In the settlement afterwards, Paraguay lost 142,500 square kilometres (55,000 square miles) of territory to Brazil, Uruguay and Argentina.

Juan Manuel de Rosas depicted in a portrait commissioned before his overthrow in 1853.

Coups and juntas

Apart from the *caudillos*, the most commonly found form of dictatorship in Latin America was a military one. This was because the armed forces were generally the strongest, most well-organised branch of government on the continent. When a national crisis loomed it was invariably the army that intervened, deposing the civilian government and taking control of the country in an act known as a *coup d'état* (a French phrase, literally meaning a 'stroke of state'). Following this intervention a small group of military leaders, known as a *junta* (Spanish for 'council'), would rule the country, with one of its members taking on the role of supreme leader.

ANTONIO LOPEZ DE SANTA ANNA (1794–1876)

Born in Mexico in 1794, Santa Anna played a central role in the creation of the modern state of Mexico. As a young officer he took part in a revolt against Spain which led to the establishment of the republic of Mexico in 1823. Then he successfully resisted Spanish attempts to recapture its colony. Santa Anna was elected president in 1833. Although he lost the territory of Texas to the USA, he prevented the French from occupying his country, and even lost a leg in the fighting. Over the next fifteen years he twice declared himself dictator of Mexico, and was twice deposed and exiled – largely because of his harsh, authoritarian style of government. In his late seventies, Santa Anna was allowed to return to Mexico, where he died in poverty in 1876.

This urge to intervene in politics was especially powerful among Latin American armed forces leaders because they often had very little else to do. Unlike the European powers, for example, who were wary of one another and had colonial wars to wage, the armies of Latin America were keen to seize the chance of some action.

This pattern of military intervention, however, greatly affected the stability and development of Latin America. A *coup* may have provided a short-term solution to a national crisis, but successive *coups* made it difficult for most Latin American countries to establish any continuity of government. Staging *coups* also became a habit that was hard to break: Bolivia, for example, has seen more than sixty since winning independence from Spain in 1825.

The tradition of dictatorship has considerably hampered Latin America's ability to develop stable and prosperous societies. Today, most countries in the continent remain deeply divided, with a small wealthy élite and a vast population of poor urban and rural workers.

During one of the most brutal coups of the late twentieth century, troops under the command of General Pinochet guard pro-government prisoners held in a sports stadium in Santiago, Chile, in 1973.

Authoritarianism in Europe

Europe, too, had its authoritarian dictators before the rise of the totalitarians. Among them was Josef Pilsudski of Poland. Following a successful military career he was made first president of newly independent Poland in 1918. His term of office ended in 1922. In 1926 he led a military *coup* against the government because he felt it was not offering Poland the strong leadership it needed. From then on, until his death in 1935, Pilsudski ruled Poland as a virtual dictator. His main ambition was to guarantee Polish independence from the two powerful nations on either side of her border – Soviet Russia and Nazi Germany. Before he died he arranged non-aggression pacts with both of these totalitarian regimes, whereby all three countries promised not to attack one another. Pilsudski's pacts with Hitler and Stalin were not honoured, however. In 1939 the Nazis and the Soviets occupied Poland, and agreed to divide it between them.

Another European authoritarian dictator was Antonio de Oliviera Salazar, who ruled Portugal for more than thirty years. Salazar rose to power in 1932 and was only replaced as leader of his country in 1968, when he suffered a stroke which rendered him unable to continue in office. Salazar established a so-called *Estado Novo* (New State) in Portugal, which had much in common with the fascist dictatorship of Mussolini in Italy. Under the watchful eye of a state secret police, all opposing political parties were banned, trade unions were forbidden, and the media came under strict government control. Although politically sympathetic to Mussolini and Hitler, Salazar ensured that Portugal remained neutral during the Second World War. As his country was not defeated by the Allies, this ensured that Salazar remained in power after the war. Subsequently, Salazar attempted to hold on to Portugal's dwindling African empire by fighting unpopular and wasteful wars against liberation movements in Mozambique and Angola.

ERNST FÖRSTER
WIEN · KARLSBAD

General Josef Clemens Pilsudski, first president of Poland, and one of Europe's first dictators, shown here in around 1920.

Doomed foreign policy

Josef Pilsudski was pessimistic about the value of his non-aggression pacts with Poland's hostile neighbours. In the year before he died he speculated that his 1934 pact with Nazi Germany would merely transform Poland 'from Germany's *hors d'oeuvre* [starter] to her dessert.' It was an astute observation. The Nazis invaded Poland only after they had absorbed Austria and conquered Czechoslovakia.

The Father of the Turks

After the First World War, the inefficient and corrupt Ottoman Empire collapsed. In its place emerged the state of Turkey. The Ottoman Empire had been steeped in the past, and Turkish general Mustafa Kemal was determined to transform his country into a modern nation. Declared president in 1923 he ruled as a dictator, permitting no opposition to his sweeping reforms.

The country's education system, transport network and industry were improved. The Muslim religion, which had hitherto dominated life in the region, was kept out of politics and education. Turkey adopted the Western calendar and alphabet. Women were encouraged to take a more active role in society and were given the vote. Kemal became known as Ataturk, meaning the Father of the Turks. Although he was a dictator, his ultimate ambition for Turkey was that the country should become a democracy. He died in 1938 and remains a great national hero. The country is still divided, however, on the issue of how much control the Muslim religion should have on the daily life of Turkey.

Mustafa Kemal – seen here in the centre of the photograph with hat in hand – reviews Turkish troops in Constantinople in 1926.

Rule or die!

The Islamic Ottoman Empire lasted for more than six hundred years. At its height, in the 1680s, it controlled territory from Budapest and the Ukraine, south to Baghdad, and almost all the African coast along the Mediterranean. The Empire was ruled by a hereditary monarchy known as the Sultanate. Between 1300 and 1603 it was traditional for the new sultan (who was chosen by the ruling sultan from among his sons just before his death) immediately to execute all his brothers. This was to avoid civil wars breaking out between brothers who were squabbling for the right to succeed their father. As a method of seizing and holding on to absolute power, it makes even the most ruthless dictator seem mild by comparison.

CHAPTER 3

Totalitarian Dictators

Few tyrants in history could equal the two greatest dictators of the twentieth century – Adolf Hitler and Joseph Stalin. Although both men were supposedly at opposite ends of the political spectrum – Hitler was a fascist and Stalin was a communist – they controlled regimes which had much in common with each other. In fact they were so alike that the political term 'totalitarian' can be applied to both of them. Totalitarian means that the government rules and regulates every aspect of life in a country.

The Soviet dictator Stalin (right) with Lenin, who had actually led the communists to power in 1917. This photo was used by Stalin in 1936 to suggest that friendly relations had always existed between the two men. The photo was, in reality, a montage of two separate images.

The rise to power of Stalin

Stalin did not lead his party into government in Russia. He inherited his position from Vladimir Ilyich Lenin, the leader of the Bolshevik Party who had seized power from the Provisional Government in the second Russian Revolution of November 1917. The Bolsheviks set about creating the world's first communist state, and renamed the country the Soviet Union. From the moment the Bolsheviks seized power, Russia moved towards a one-party totalitarian regime. This was not very different from the rule of the tsar, who had been a hereditary monarch with complete control over the military and the Russian citizens. The Bolsheviks, however, were far more ruthless in imposing their will, and did so with much greater efficiency.

Lenin and Stalin worked closely together before and after the revolution. At first, Lenin had a high regard for the hard-working and cunning Stalin, and regarded him as a possible successor. But towards the end of his life Lenin began to feel that Stalin was too rude and ruthless to take over from him. When Lenin died in 1924, the Soviet Union was governed by a triumvirate (three people), including Stalin. However, by 1928, Stalin had established himself as sole leader.

A nation in poverty

Stalin visited unbelievable horrors on his people, the like of which would never have been tolerated in a democracy. However, unlike his fellow tyrant Hitler whose actions were prompted by greed for territory and racial hatred, Stalin perhaps had a more rational reason for his actions. When the Bolsheviks seized power in Russia in 1917, they inherited a vast but underdeveloped, agrarian and largely pre-industrial country.

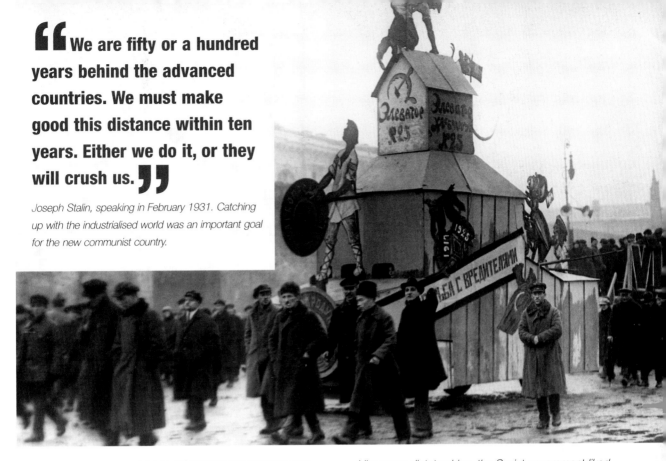

> **"**We are fifty or a hundred years behind the advanced countries. We must make good this distance within ten years. Either we do it, or they will crush us.**"**

Joseph Stalin, speaking in February 1931. Catching up with the industrialised world was an important goal for the new communist country.

Like many dictatorships, the Soviet government liked to put on a parade. Here, in 1925, workers march through the streets of a Russian city to celebrate the anniversary of the revolution.

JOSEPH STALIN

Born in Georgia in 1879, Josif Dzhugashvili was the son of a shoemaker. The great dictator began calling himself 'Stalin' (man of steel) in 1912. As a Georgian rather than a Russian speaker, Stalin always believed himself to be an outsider in Moscow. He only learned Russian at the age of nine and spoke it with a heavy accent all his life. Compared with other revolutionary leaders, such as Lenin and Trotsky, he was also quite uneducated. Soviet propaganda presented him as a benign and caring uncle, and he was adored by millions of ordinary Russians. But those closest to him soon learned he had a paranoid and unpredictable character. He inspired an almost hysterical fear in his colleagues, who he often had executed for no rational reason. For example, in 1939, when he mispronounced the word 'agriculture' during a conference speech, all subsequent speakers pronounced it the same way as him, for fear of drawing attention to his poor Russian grammar and thereby falling from favour.

Living conditions in Russia were almost medieval in comparison with those of its wealthy Western neighbours. In the countryside, millions of peasants struggled to survive in squalor and poverty. At the time of the Revolution, many were escaping their farms and villages to live in overcrowded slums in towns and cities, where they found poorly paid work in Russia's newly developing industries. The people, as a whole, had no previous experience of democracy. Authoritarian government had been part of Russian life since the fourteenth century. Most Russians would have perceived little difference between their new Soviet masters and the previous rule of the tsars.

During the 1920s and 1930s, the Soviet Union embarked on a far-reaching programme of industrialisation. Factories, power stations, steel works, hydro-electric dams and other technological necessities for a modern nation were created, all of which the Soviet Union had largely lacked. In a decade or so, this policy of industrialisation achieved what other nations such as France and Britain had taken fifty or a hundred years to build. This extraordinary feat was accomplished partly through the use of slave labour – comprised mainly of political prisoners who had fallen foul of the Soviet regime.

More disastrous for the Soviet Union was Stalin's plan to transform its means of food production. The country's agricultural base was made up of thousands of small farms run by peasants known as *kulaks*. Stalin intended to reorganise these farms into larger state-run collective farms. The *kulaks* resisted this fiercely, and were executed in their thousands under Stalin's orders. In protest, the peasants destroyed crops and killed livestock. Their actions, together with the disruption caused by transforming small farms into collective farms, led to a food shortage. Famine swept across parts of the Soviet Union. Some historians believe that up to ten million people died between 1932 and 1933 while Stalin tried to enforce his policy of collectivisation.

Just as sinister were a series of 'purges' carried out directly on Stalin's orders during the 1930s. Millions of Russians, mainly Communist Party members, government workers, army officers and university staff were suspected of not being loyal supporters of the Soviet regime. They were arrested and many thousands were shot. Millions more were sent to forced labour camps where they were worked to death.

❝I did not enter a single inhabited room, even the humblest and the most sordid, without (noticing) a portrait of Stalin, hanging on the wall…❞

French novelist, dramatist and diarist André Gide describing a visit to the Soviet Union during the 1930s.

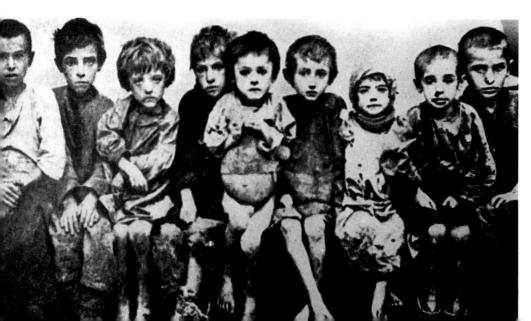

This photo shows a handful of the millions of Soviet citizens who suffered under Stalin during the 1930s. These starving children are orphans, the victims of famine following the failure of the collectivisation of Soviet farms.

A Soviet soldier waves a red flag following the victory at Stalingrad in 1943.

An ill wind

Despite the suffering and untold numbers of deaths, some of Stalin's drastic policies probably saved the Soviet Union from the only regime in the world more barbaric and ruthless than his own. In 1941, Nazi Germany invaded from the west, intending to turn the area of the Soviet Union on the European border into a German colony, and the Soviets into slaves. Organised by their own fiercely repressive government, the Soviet people fought back with great bravery and tenacity. After the first six months of the war, when Moscow and Leningrad (now St Petersburg) were nearly captured, tanks and other armaments from Russia's new factories began to make their presence felt. Following the battle of Stalingrad, which took place during the winter of 1942–43, the Soviets forced the German army into an almost constant retreat, which only stopped at the German capital of Berlin.

Stalin's dictatorship had enabled the Soviet Union to defeat its greatest enemy. When the war ended, Soviet troops were in control of the entire eastern half of Europe. Stalin feared another attack from the west; after all, Western nations had invaded Russia three times during the previous twenty-one years – Germany in

TIMELINE: THE RISE OF THE DICTATORS – 1920s AND 1930s

1922
Mussolini seizes power in Italy and rules as fascist dictator until 1945

1923
Hitler tries to seize power in Germany in the Beer Hall Putsch in Munich. He fails, and is imprisoned.

1924
Lenin, leader of the Soviet Union, dies and a struggle for leadership begins

1928
Stalin establishes himself as sole leader of the Soviet Union. His great rival Trotsky is exiled and later assassinated.

1929
The Wall Street Crash leads to worldwide economic depression and rise of Nazi Party in Germany

1932
Famine sweeps across the Soviet Union as communist collective farm policies fail

1933
The Nazi Party comes to power in Germany and immediately sweeps away democratic government

1934
Hitler's rivals within the Nazi Party are eliminated during the 'Night of the Long Knives'

1936
Purges begin in Soviet Union. Millions are imprisoned or executed.

1939
Franco becomes fascist dictator of Spain. Hitler invades Poland, setting the Second World War in motion.

1941
Hitler invades the Soviet Union in the greatest clash of arms the world has ever known

1920   1930   1940

> ## " Artists are engineers of the human soul. "

Stalin mixes politics and art on 26 October, 1932. This quote illustrates his belief – characteristic of totalitarian dictators – that every aspect of life ought to serve the dictator's philosophy. Stalin thought that even art should direct the people's thoughts to a greater understanding and appreciation of the Soviet state.

The human cost of Stalin's rule
One figure estimates that perhaps one in five of all Soviet citizens, including those killed in the war, died during Stalin's time in power. Even historians sympathetic to the Soviet communist regime accept that almost 600,000 people were executed during the purges of 1937 and 1938, and that by the time of Stalin's death in 1953 more than five-and-a-half million Soviet citizens had been imprisoned in forced labour camps.

1914, the Allies in 1918 and Germany again in 1941. Stalin therefore decided to maintain an army presence in Eastern Europe. A mighty Soviet empire stretched eastwards from Berlin and the borders of West Germany to the Bering Straits in the North Pacific.

Stalin's legacy

Did Stalin's dictatorship bring the Soviet people any other benefits, apart from that of repelling the German invasion? It is difficult to say. Most Russians had lived in great poverty and illiterate ignorance before the Revolution of 1917. Within two decades, the Soviet government managed to create a strong industrial nation with a considerable increase in opportunities for people from humble backgrounds. By the time Stalin died in 1953, the Soviet people were undoubtedly better educated, provided for, and cared for (by a national health system) than they had ever been before.

Nevertheless, the Soviet people had paid a terrible price for these benefits. Stalin's rule had resulted in the deaths of millions. In the long term, the totalitarian system he established became stale and corrupt. After his death he was succeeded by increasingly dull and unimaginative leaders in what became known as 'the era of stagnation'. These men lacked Stalin's cruelty and ruthlessness, but they inherited and wielded power through the systems he had established. Any criticism of the Soviet government and its policies was still punishable by persecution and imprisonment.

The rise to power of Adolf Hitler

The other great dictator of the twentieth century, Adolf Hitler, brought triumph then disaster to his country. Within a decade of his coming to power in 1933, Germany had become a conquering nation that controlled an empire stretching from the French Atlantic to the Caucasus Mountains on the edge of Asiatic Russia. But by 1945 Hitler was dead, and his nation defeated and in ruins.

Unlike the Bolsheviks, who seized power as Russia descended into anarchy during the First World War, Hitler and his Nazi (National Socialist) Party were democratically elected. A founder member in 1920 of the Nazi Party, Hitler had led it since 1921. He had a gift for public speaking, and his extreme political ideas slowly gained support among the German people. Hitler preached that Germans were a 'master race' of superior human beings. It was their destiny, he said, to rule over the 'inferior' Slavic nations of the east, such as Poland and Soviet Russia. He also believed that communism and the Jewish people were Germany's greatest enemies and both should be destroyed, perhaps because both were international in nature, with no loyalty to the state.

In the early 1930s, the Great Depression swept across the world, bringing record levels of unemployment. During this time, the Nazi Party came close to winning elections in Germany. In 1932, nearly six million people were out of work, and many of them supported the Nazis because they promised to rebuild Germany and its economy. Many conservative politicians in Germany were also attracted to the Nazis. This was mainly because they opposed German communists, who they feared would lead a revolution much like the one that had occurred in Russia. In 1933 the German leader, Chancellor Fritz von Papen and his Catholic Centre Party suggested that Hitler form a government with them.

Adolf Hitler, accompanied by his deputy Rudolph Hess, reviews a massive parade held to honour the Nazi Party and its leader in Nuremberg, Germany, in 1941.

> **Every child says 'Heil Hitler!' from 50 to 150 times a day…. The formula is required by law; if you meet a friend on the way to school, you say it; study periods are opened and closed with 'Heil Hitler!', 'Heil Hitler!' says the postman, the street-car conductor, the girl who sells you notebooks at the stationery store; and if your parents' first words when you come home to lunch are not 'Heil Hitler!' they have been guilty of a punishable offence, and can be denounced.**

An extract from Erika Mann's book School for Barbarians, *about life in Nazi Germany.*

At the time, the Nazis had the greatest number of seats in the Reichstag (the German parliament), but did not have an overall majority (in other words, they could still be outvoted by an alliance of other parties). Once in government, Hitler outmanoeuvred his political allies, and he and the Nazis were soon in complete control.

Nazi rule

Once in power, Hitler and his fellow Nazi leaders used their new authority to sweep away any opposition, both inside and outside the party. Extreme measures, even murder, were used to bring dissenters to heel. Those opponents left alive were imprisoned in brutal concentration camps such as Dachau, which were set up within weeks of the Nazis coming to power in 1933.

At first, Hitler's policies brought prosperity. People who had previously been unemployed were given jobs in factories making weapons for Germany's armed forces, and on new public building programmes and motorway construction. Hitler began to claim back land that many Germans felt had been unfairly taken from Germany at the end of the

German troops in Paris, France, in 1940. Between 1939 and 1942, Hitler's armies conquered almost all of Europe.

First World War. In 1939, Hitler declared war on Poland as part of his policy of seizing territory on Germany's eastern border. In response, Britain and France declared war on Germany, and the Second World War began. Although Germany conquered vast swathes of territory at the start of the war, within three years Hitler was fighting an impossible battle against the two greatest powers on earth – the USA and the Soviet Union. By 1945, Germany was crushed and millions of German people had been killed. In a post-war pact between the victorious Allies, the country was divided into East and West Germany.

Jews and other 'enemies' of the Nazis were worked and starved to death in concentration camps like this one at Buchenwald, Germany.

The Final Solution

When the Second World War broke out, more than eight million Jews came under Nazi rule. Hitler singled the Jews out as a specific target of racial hatred and ordered that they should be exterminated. This was what the Nazis referred to as their 'Final Solution' to the 'Jewish problem'. At first, all Jews under Nazi control were rounded up and made to live and work in walled-in ghettos, which they were not allowed to leave. They were also made to wear the Star of David on their clothes to identify them as Jews. Special execution squads were sent to the conquered eastern territories to eliminate the Jews. When this proved to be too time-consuming, Hitler introduced an unprecedented programme of systematised murder, and ordered the building of death camps where Jews could be gassed and disposed of quickly in their hundreds of thousands. Altogether, around six million were killed. Only a totalitarian dictator could have carried out such a monstrous act with virtually no opposition.

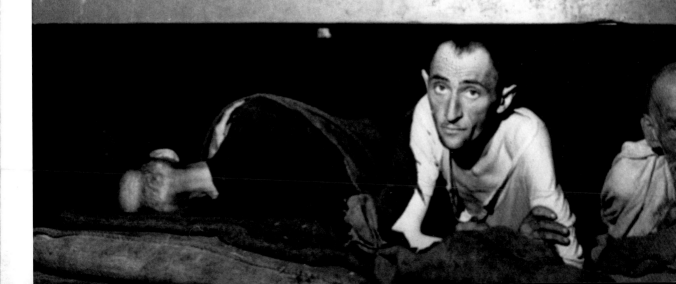

Life under the heel of the dictators

In spite of their obvious differences, Nazi Germany and the Soviet Union had much in common. Their leaders were portrayed by the regimes that supported them as almost god-like entities. Over time, their parties and their charismatic personalities came to represent the very essence of the countries they ruled.

Both regimes used blatant propaganda to great effect. The media was completely controlled by the government. Newspapers, radio broadcasts and newsreels (news programmes shown in cinemas) only reported on events in a way that showed the government in a positive light; negative or critical reporting was banned. As far as cinema was concerned, films might be about frivolous subjects but they still had to conform to the ideals of the Nazi or Soviet regime. For example, a romance made in Nazi Germany would never show a love affair between a German and a Jewish or black person because these were racial types considered inferior to Germans. In the Soviet Union, in a movement that became known as 'Socialist Realism', Stalin's government declared that every piece of art – from an orchestral symphony to a painting – had to 'educate workers in the spirit of communism'.

" The broad mass of the nation will more easily fall victim to a big lie than to a small one. "

From Adolf Hitler's political biography, Mein Kampf. In this quote Hitler discusses the process of lying as a way of winning the support of the population and gaining power.

Snaring citizens

Both regimes also liked to involve their citizens in great parades and rallies. In Nazi Germany, massive rallies were held in sports stadiums, often at night and lit by torches carried by thousands of uniformed marchers. At these rallies, Hitler and other top Nazis would make impassioned speeches and the atmosphere would be wildly nationalistic and hysterical, with the audience behaving in a frenzied way similar to that of fans at a pop concert today.

Hitler and Stalin both made the most of the unquestioning obedience of children by fostering youth organisations that encouraged the political indoctrination of boys and girls. (Indoctrination means teaching beliefs and attitudes in a way that does not encourage any questioning of what is being taught.) In Soviet Russia, children were expected to join a youth group called the Young Pioneers. In Nazi Germany, the Hitler Youth and League of German Maidens were created specifically with the intention of producing loyal and obedient Nazi citizens. In Germany and the Soviet Union, schools had to make sure that pupils were educated with lessons that reflected the political opinions of the regime. Most sinister of all, young people were taught that ultimately their loyalty lay with the state. They were even encouraged to report their parents to the police, if they overheard them making anti-Nazi or anti-Soviet remarks.

Last resort

So effective was Soviet and Nazi propaganda that Hitler and Stalin were adored by the majority of their subjects. Pictures and posters glorifying the leaders could be found in almost every home. If all else failed, however, the totalitarian dictators had one final trick up their sleeves to command obedience from their people – terror. Hitler and Stalin relied on a secret police force to monitor and arrest any opponents. The Germans had the Gestapo (the secret

In this poster from the Second World War, figures from Russia's pre-revolutionary past urge Soviet soldiers to defend their motherland against the invading Nazis.

Death sentence

In Nazi Germany, telling anti-Hitler jokes was sufficient to send a person to the firing squad. For example, Nazi People's Court judge, Hans Joachim Rehse, ordered the execution of a priest who had told an anti-Hitler joke to an electrician working at his parsonage.

ЕМСЯ МЫ ЗДОРОВО
ЛЕМ ОТЧАЯННО –
УКИ СУВОРОВА,

state police), the Russians the NKVD (the People's Commissariat of Internal Affairs), and both were infamous for their cruelty and ruthlessness. Their reputation was carefully fostered. A population terrified by its own government was an easy one to control. In Nazi Germany and Soviet Russia, opposition was punishable by death.

Hitler's murderous policies were carried out with very little opposition. Here, German soldiers take part in a massacre of Jews in Warsaw, Poland, in 1940.

Lesser lights

Other dictators also came to power in Europe during the 1920s and 1930s. Most prominent among them were Benito Mussolini of Italy and Francisco Franco of Spain. Their regimes followed similar styles to those of Hitler and Stalin, but they never gained the same degree of power and notoriety of the two great dictators.

Mussolini came to power in Italy in 1922. At the time, the country was in economic chaos and rent by violent clashes between fascists and communists. A former schoolteacher who led the fascists, Mussolini was 'invited' by the Italian king, Victor Emmanuel III, to form a government. In fact, the king had little choice: the fascists had demanded that the government be turned over to them, and Mussolini and four other fascist leaders had marched on Rome with their troops when the government had not relented. Italy's youngest prime minister, Mussolini was to rule the country for the next twenty years. Strict censorship was imposed on the Italian media, where Mussolini was portrayed as a great hero, inspiring Italians to create 'a new Roman Empire'. The Italian fascists wore distinctive black uniforms and held great parades at which Mussolini would make dramatic speeches. Mussolini tolerated no opposition and had his political rivals killed. His fascist organisation and style of leadership were a great inspiration to Hitler, but his rule was ultimately less devastating than that of the Nazis.

The Second World War proved to be Mussolini's undoing. In 1937, Hitler and Mussolini forged a military alliance and Italy's population was dragged unwillingly into Nazi Germany's wars of conquest. Almost every battle the Italian army fought was a disaster and, in 1943, Mussolini was eventually deposed by his own government. Rescued by Nazi paratroopers, he survived until 1945 but was executed at the end of the war by Italian partisans.

The Italian dictator Benito Mussolini, shown here making an impassioned speech during the 1930s, was greatly admired by Hitler. The two men made allies of each other's countries, with disastrous consequences for both.

❝❞ Blood alone moves the wheels of history. ❝❞

❝❞ Fascism is a religion. The twentieth century will be known as the century of fascism. ❝❞

Two of the dramatic slogans that were a feature of Benito Mussolini's speech-making.

General Franco

Francisco Franco was one of the three great fascist dictators of Europe, and a natural ally to Hitler and Mussolini. Unlike them, he survived the Second World War. Franco came to prominence in 1936, following the election of a radical left-wing government in Spain. This socialist government's existence was a cause of grave concern to the deeply conservative members of Spain's upper class and army. Civil war soon broke out. Franco and other army generals led the resistance against government forces. After a brutal three-year struggle they triumphed, toppled the government, and Franco became dictator of Spain. Political opponents were massacred and all opposition was banned. Although he voiced his support for his fellow fascist dictators, Franco astutely avoided joining forces with them, and Spain remained neutral during the Second World War.

Until his death in 1975 Franco remained in power, ruling a repressive and deeply conservative Spain – a strange relic from the years before the war. Following Franco's death, Spain returned to democracy and established a constitutional monarchy along lines similar to those of the United Kingdom.

The Spanish dictator Francisco Franco shown here at a parade with Hitler (far left). Despite receiving help from the Nazis during Spain's civil war, Franco was shrewd enough not to give military support to Germany during the Second World War.

CHAPTER 4
Cold War Dictators

After the horrors unleashed by Hitler and Stalin, it is perhaps surprising that the years following the Second World War saw further dictatorships emerge. The reasons for this lie in the two ideas that dominated politics during the second half of the twentieth century: the Cold War (*see below*), and the idea of a world divided into three parts (*see page 31*). Most of the dictators from this post-war era did not have as much power and influence as Hitler and Stalin. The countries they controlled were usually too small or poor to be a threat to anyone other than their immediate neighbours. Nevertheless, the people living under these dictators suffered the consequences of their rule.

Cold War

When the Second World War ended, many of the world's countries split into two armed camps, lining up behind the only superpowers – the USA and the Soviet Union. Between 1945 and 1991, the Cold War prevailed. This was an era of great hostility and mistrust during which the two sides threatened each other with invasion at best and nuclear annihilation at worst.

Those countries that allied themselves with the USA, principally the UK, the countries of Western Europe, and most other nations outside the control of the Soviet Union, did so largely of their own free will or because the USA supported their governments financially and, on occasion, militarily. Those that allied themselves with the Soviet Union often had little choice in the matter. These consisted of those countries in Eastern Europe that had been occupied by the Soviets at the end of the Second World War, and where communist-style regimes had been set up regardless of local wishes. These countries were known as 'buffer states', and the Soviet Union used them to protect itself from further invasion from Western Europe. The Soviets had been invaded three times from

Hot and cold
The Cold War was so-called to distinguish it from a 'hot' war, where there is actual fighting between two hostile nations. In place of open warfare, the methods used by countries fighting the Cold War consisted of propaganda, threats, economic sanctions and espionage (spying).

During a visit to Berlin, Germany, in 1963, US President John F. Kennedy (on the podium) looks over the infamous Wall, which became a symbol of the inhumanity of Eastern Europe's communist dictatorships.

the west since 1914 and were determined it should not occur again. In addition to the buffer states, the Soviets had some allies further afield, including Cuba to whom they provided financial aid, trade, and military assistance.

For more than forty years, until the collapse of the Soviet Union in 1991, most of the world was divided into the two political camps of West and East. The divide was further complicated by the emergence of another communist superpower, China – a vast but poor nation containing one fifth of the entire population of the globe. Fortunately for the non-communist nations, China and the Soviet Union soon developed a difficult and guarded relationship towards each other and never succeeded in presenting a united front to their capitalist opponents.

Three different worlds

As the Cold War progressed, Western political commentators came to see the world as divided into three main economic blocs. There was the First World of prosperous capitalist nations – principally the USA, Western Europe and other so-called 'developed nations', such as Canada and Australia. This was also broadly referred to as 'the West'. These First-World countries were mainly ones with a democratic tradition – that is, they had a long history of free speech and free elections.

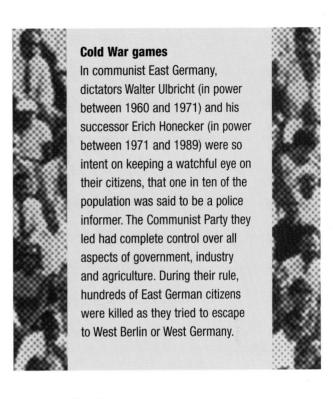

Cold War games
In communist East Germany, dictators Walter Ulbricht (in power between 1960 and 1971) and his successor Erich Honecker (in power between 1971 and 1989) were so intent on keeping a watchful eye on their citizens, that one in ten of the population was said to be a police informer. The Communist Party they led had complete control over all aspects of government, industry and agriculture. During their rule, hundreds of East German citizens were killed as they tried to escape to West Berlin or West Germany.

The next bloc was the Second World, consisting principally of the communist nations of the Soviet Union, Eastern Europe and China. This was broadly referred to as 'the East'. These Second-World nations had one-party communist rule where personal freedom was restricted. Those people opposed to the government were persecuted or imprisoned.

Finally there was the Third World. This consisted of most of the countries in Asia, Africa and Latin America which were mainly poor and 'developing' or 'underdeveloped' – meaning they did not have the industrial wealth of the First or Second Worlds. The Third World was controlled by an assortment of different styles of government. Although it was a common political expression in the 1960s and 70s, especially among nations that had recently divested themselves of their colonial past, the term 'Third World' has fallen from favour and now tends to be viewed as patronising.

The USA and the Soviet Union were concerned that their Third World friends should not 'go over to the other side'. So, when the two main superpowers looked for allies in the Third World, they were keen to reward support with economic aid. A political climate therefore developed in which dictatorship thrived because dictators held on to their positions with the support of their superpower backers.

A protester in Prague, Czechoslovakia, urges Soviet troops to do their worst, during the uprising of 1968.

Shoe mania

For most of the Cold War, the USA supported the anti-communist dictator of the Philippines, Ferdinand Marcos. Originally democratically elected in 1965, Marcos suspended the Philippine constitution in 1972 and ruled as a dictator – murdering political opponents and allowing his country to fall into economic decay. After Marcos was deposed in 1986, it was discovered that he had acquired a personal fortune of $352 million – most of it from his impoverished country. His wife, Imelda, was reported to own 3,000 pairs of shoes. When questioned about this, she angrily retorted that she only had 1,060!

In turn, the two superpowers were determined to establish or prop up regimes that would guarantee them support. The Soviet Union did this mainly by force – all the Eastern European regimes of the Cold War were set up specifically to extend support for the Soviet Union. Any rebellions by the local population or government — such as the uprisings in Hungary in 1956 and in Czechoslovakia in 1968 — were crushed by military force. The subversive actions of the USA were often more subtle than this. They included undermining regimes unsympathetic to the West by giving secret help to their opponents (for example, in Chile in the 1970s), and withdrawing trade or economic assistance (for example, from Cuba after the communist revolution of the 1950s).

Dictators in the East

In the countries of Eastern Europe, communist leaders loyal to the Soviet Union ruled with dictator-like powers. Although they varied in style, some, such as President Ceauçescu of Romania, carried out the kind of social engineering generally associated with totalitarian regimes. In the mid-1980s, Ceauçescu introduced the policy of 'systemisation' in an attempt to modernise his country. In the capital, Bucharest, up to one-fifth of the houses in residential areas were knocked down and replaced with modern, high-rise apartment blocks. Whole villages were destroyed and their inhabitants placed in similar drab, modern housing complexes. The reasons for this were to remove the link with Romania's non-communist past and make the inhabitants of these new dwellings easier to monitor and control. Ceauçescu planned to relocate up to eleven million people in this way. His policy was only stopped when he was deposed and executed in 1989.

Third-World dictators

Until the Second World War, many nations in Africa and Asia had been colonies – countries controlled by European nations such as France and Britain. After the war, most of these countries gained their independence. Initially, a democratic system of government was usually introduced based on the system that operated in the country of the former colonial ruler. But these fledgling democracies almost always failed. Poverty, conflicts between different tribal groups, and rivalries between different regions and religions meant that most of them could not prosper or survive. As they descended into chaos, these embryonic democracies were replaced by dictatorships. In some countries (for example, Ghana under Kwame Nkrumah), the elected president or prime minister simply banned any opposition and established single-party rule. In others, army officers (for example, Idi Amin in Uganda) seized power.

Turning a blind eye

Almost all of these new dictators flourished with the help of the USA, Soviet Union or China. In the tense climate of the Cold War, what mattered most to the superpowers was the reliability of these dictators as allies. The murderous and often deeply corrupt rule of

During the 1970s, African dictator Idi Amin was one of many army officers who seized power from a weak civilian government in post-colonial Africa.

President Bokassa of the Central African Republic, seen here during his infamously expensive coronation ceremony in 1977.

many of them appeared to be of lesser importance. This edgy political climate allowed dictators to thrive. For example, President Haile Mariam Mengistu was the leader of a military *junta* that ruled Ethiopia during the 1970s and 1980s. Mengistu gave orders for the imprisonment, torture and execution of thousands of opponents, and conducted a civil war against rival forces that led to the death by starvation of millions of his people. Despite this, the Soviet Union supported him with economic aid and armaments. When the Soviet regime collapsed in 1991, Mengistu fled to Zimbabwe and currently lives in exile under the protection of another dictator, Robert Mugabe.

President Bokassa of the Central African Republic came to power in a *coup* of 1966. He was supported by the French government which wanted to ensure that his country's supply of uranium would be available for the French nuclear weapons programme. Bokassa presided over a cruel, oppressive regime, and siphoned off foreign aid intended for his desperately poor country. In 1977, he declared himself Emperor Bokassa I and spent $20 million on his coronation – a figure equal to a third of his country's annual income. In 1979, Bokassa's excesses caught up with him and his French allies acted to remove him from power. Following a well-publicised massacre of civilians in which Bokassa was alleged to have taken part, he was deposed in another *coup*, backed by French army soldiers.

Toppling democracy

In 1970, the USA became greatly alarmed by the coming to power of the world's first freely elected communist government in Latin America. Chile's new leader, Salvador Allende, pushed through a series of policies designed to turn the country into a democratic socialist country, with a state-controlled industry. The USA was especially concerned that Allende might become a natural ally of the Soviet Union, thus increasing communist influence in a continent that was one of the USA's most immediate neighbours.

There was considerable resistance to Allende's radical policies among Chile's richer citizens, and among institutions such as the armed forces. The USA took advantage of this and gave secret assistance to Allende's opponents in planning and carrying out an armed rebellion. The result was a military *coup* in September 1973, in the wake of which General Augusto Pinochet, a brutal dictator, was installed as Chile's president. Allende and around 15,000 people were killed. Pinochet banned all opposition to his rule, and used strict censorship and a secret police force to remain in power. In response, around one-tenth of Chileans emigrated. Nevertheless Pinochet's regime received US aid and support, because it was seen as an ally against communism. In 1988, Pinochet was eventually voted out of power; although he left office, he remained commander-in-chief of the army.

His face showing signs of strain, Chilean president Salvador Allende reviews the troops that will shortly be deployed to overthrow him. Allende was killed in a military coup which toppled his elected socialist government in 1973.

FIDEL CASTRO (1927–)

In 1959, the communist leader Fidel Castro came to power in Cuba after fighting to depose a corrupt dictator named Fulgencio Batista. Cuba had previously been a very poor country with a few wealthy businesses, many of which had US owners or backers. By seizing the wealth of these businesses, Castro provoked the USA into banning trade with Cuba. The USA also supported an invasion by pro-Batista Cuban exiles, which failed. This took place in 1961 in a part of coastal Cuba known as the Bay of Pigs. Castro turned to the Soviet Union for help, and Soviet aid and trade soon became vital to Cuba's economy. However, even after the collapse of Soviet communism, Castro remained in power. Cuba today is considerably poorer than it was, but has begun to build up its prosperity through tourism. This in spite of the fact that the USA continues its economic and tourist embargo, and despite the end of the Cold War.

1960 As thousands flee from communist rule in East Berlin, East German dictator Walter Ulbricht orders the building of the Berlin Wall

1961 US-backed Cuban exiles invade their island at the Bay of Pigs in an unsuccessful bid to depose the pro-Soviet dictator Fidel Castro

1973 Fearing increased Soviet influence in South America, the US government helps to overthrow the democratically elected socialist government in Chile. President Allende is killed and replaced by the brutal, pro-US dictatorship of General Augusto Pinochet.

1960　1965　1970　1975　1980

TIMELINE: COLD WAR DICTATORS, 1960–1980

1972 Despite human rights violations and corruption charges, Philippine anti-communist dictator Ferdinand Marcos receives US backing

1977 Pro-Western dictator Jean Bedel Bokassa of the Central African Republic outrages the world by spending a third of his country's annual income on his own coronation as emperor. He is deposed in 1979 with the help of French army soldiers.

CHAPTER 5

Dictatorship in the Modern World

he end of the Cold War transformed the world's political landscape. When the communist regime in the Soviet Union collapsed, the Eastern European dictatorships it had created and maintained collapsed with it. As for the West, it no longer needed to tolerate oppressive and transparently evil regimes that were 'on its side'. Government policymakers in the USA and Europe began to champion a new kind of thinking, arguing that democracy was the best hope for peace in the post-Cold War world. This new thinking was reinforced by the historically proven fact that many dictators have an irresistible urge to lead their countries into war.

(Since) August 1914 the world has gone from ten or twelve democracies to over a hundred and twenty... nothing like that has happened within a single lifetime in world history before.

James Woolsey, former director of the US Central Intelligence Agency, 2003.

Collapse of communism

In 1986, an explosion at Chernobyl, a nuclear power station in the Ukraine, highlighted many of the things that were wrong with the world's most powerful communist country. At least 32 people died and hundreds of thousands living nearby had to be resettled. Chernobyl was a disaster because it rendered the entire area around the power station unfit for human habitation, and spread radioactive pollution all around the world. At first, the Soviet government lied to its people about the scale of the disaster. Then it was revealed that the explosion had been

People in Red Square, Moscow, in May 2004. The collapse of communism has brought more personal freedom, but Russia is now a country of huge extremes dividing rich and poor.

caused by a combination of factors, among them poor quality building brought on by government pressure to construct the plant in record time, and power station managers who were so afraid of punishment they did not dare to admit that they could not keep the station working properly.

The Chernobyl disaster and its consequences led to a period of heart-searching among members of the Soviet leadership. The state they had inherited from Stalin was deeply flawed. The Soviet president at the time, Mikhail Gorbachev, announced a new policy of 'glasnost' (openness and honesty) and 'perestroika' (reform). But the Soviet system could not cope with democratic traditions such as open criticism. As Eastern European buffer states and regions within the Soviet Union rose up to demand their independence, the regime collapsed. Today, the Soviet Union no longer exists and many of its former states are now independent. Russia itself is in a state of economic turmoil, lawlessness and deep uncertainty, still recovering from the effects of communism.

As the dictatorships of Eastern Europe were swept away, new democracies emerged. As a general trend, democracy, or at least moves towards democracy, have grown in countries that previously were governed by authoritarian or totalitarian regimes.

Some of the old dictatorships have continued to thrive, however, in the post-Cold War world, especially those that had no clear dependency on either superpower. In the Middle East, Arab dictators such as President Mubarak in Egypt and Colonel Qaddafi in Libya have remained in power. Saddam Hussein of Iraq was only deposed in 2003 following a US-led invasion. Dictators are still evident in Africa,

On 15 December 2003 in Amman, Jordan, a man reads a newspaper reporting the capture of Iraq's president and dictator, Saddam Hussein. A television screen in the background shows Saddam's bearded image. The newspaper features a photo of a US official taking a swab from Saddam's mouth for identity purposes. Saddam went into hiding when his regime was overthrown by a US- and British-led invasion.

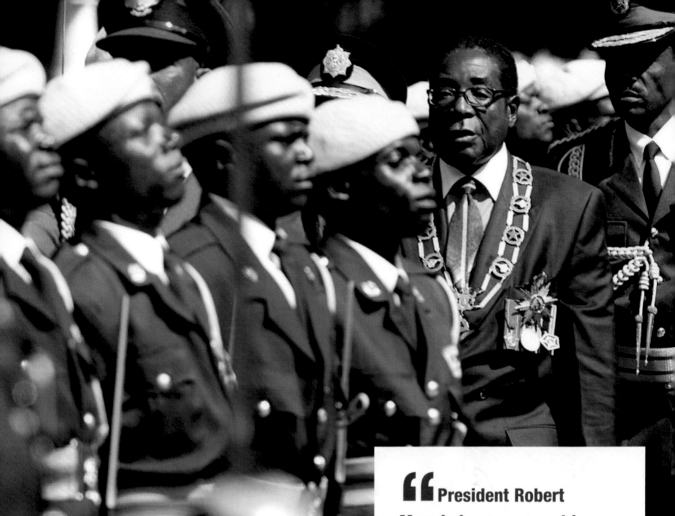

President Robert Mugabe (centre, in glasses) is the democratically elected leader of Zimbabwe. However, commentators believe that his government is now run along dictatorial lines. Here Mugabe inspects a guard of honour in July 2001.

with President Robert Mugabe of Zimbabwe perhaps one of the most notable. Although he was democratically elected in 1980, Mugabe has since clung on to power in the face of increasing opposition and rumours of torture and murder.

Fundamentalism

In the 1960s, a new style of religious dictator emerged in the Middle East. In 1969, Muammar al-Qaddafi (pronounced Gad-a-fee) came to power in Libya during a *coup* by young army officers. Qaddafi's regime bore many of the hallmarks of a

> **President Robert Mugabe's government has set up secret camps across the country in which thousands of youths are taught how to torture and kill…. The Zimbabwean government says the camps are job training centres, but those who have escaped say they are part of a brutal plan to keep Mugabe in power.**
>
> *BBC news report, 2004.*

fascist state. The government took over important areas of the economy, controlled trade unions and other organisations that represented the people of Libya, and enforced strict Islamic law.

A more extreme style of Islamic rule emerged in the last two decades of the twentieth century in the shape of the fundamentalist governments of Iran and, until 2002, Afghanistan. These regimes have been called theocracies (meaning 'government by God') because religious leaders control the country. The way in which personal behaviour has been policed in countries such as Iran and Afghanistan has led commentators to liken them to totalitarian dictatorships.

In Iran in 1980, a popular revolution overthrew the emperor or Shah, Reza Pahlavi. The Shah had followed a policy of Westernisation in Iran, along the lines set by Mustafa Kemal in Turkey. The USA had returned the Shah to power after he was briefly overthrown in 1953 by Muhammed Mosaddeq, but in 1980 the Shah was deposed once again by the Muslim cleric, Ayatollah Khomeini, who ruled Iran until his death in 1989. The Ayatollah's regime imposed strict shariah (holy) law on the country. Private conduct was regulated by a special police force. Alcohol and gambling were banned and foreign films, magazines and music were strictly vetted for any offensive material. Men and women were expected to dress modestly, a requirement that obliged all women to cover their entire bodies apart from their face and hands with a (usually) black cloak. Today, Iran has a government led by a president, Mohammed Khatemi, and a spiritual leader, Ayatollah Ali Khamenie. The country is still determined to resist attempts by opposition politicians to relax its strict religious laws. Contrary to many Western expectations, however, women in Iran have in some ways benefited from this fundamentalist regime. Considerably more women now go on to higher education and government jobs than they did under the rule of the Shah.

The Taliban

An even more oppressive regime emerged in Afghanistan in 1994. The Taliban government introduced an especially harsh interpretation of Islamic law, where women were forbidden to work and girls were not allowed to attend school. Dancing, the playing of music, sport and any other form of entertainment were forbidden. Citizens failing to observe these rules were severely punished by the country's religious police.

Dangerous haircut
Under the Taliban regime, young men who had seen the forbidden Hollywood film *Titanic* on pirate videos smuggled into the country sometimes copied Leonardo de Caprio's distinctive hairstyle. As punishment for their fashion sense, the men were beaten in the streets by the religious police and barbers who had cut their hair were closed down.

The Taliban regime that ruled Afghanistan between 1994 and 2001 insisted that all women should completely cover their bodies and faces outside the home. This form of dress is called the 'burka'.

In November 2001, the Taliban regime fell when the US military invaded Afghanistan, following the Al Qaeda-led terrorist attack on the World Trade Centre in New York City. The Taliban had openly expressed support for the Al Qaeda terrorist network, so the USA believed it necessary to bring an end to the regime in Afghanistan. Although many Afghan people were ambiguous about the US presence in their country, most were relieved to be free of the Taliban.

Vote-rigging

According to the Iraqi government, in the 2002 presidential referendum in which he was the only candidate, Saddam Hussein received 100 per cent support from his people. Bogus elections or referendums are a common feature of dictatorships. Votes are rigged, and citizens are threatened with violence if they do not vote for the dictator in question. The object of the exercise is to convince people that the dictator is a popular and just leader of his country. Today, however, with modern communications and extensive and critical media coverage this type of propaganda doesn't always succeed.

Ousting of a dictator

At the beginning of the twenty-first century Saddam Hussein was one of the most firmly entrenched dictators in the world. He rose to become president of Iraq in 1979 and displayed many of the recognisable traits of dictatorship, ruling with a brutal intolerance of any criticism and opposition. Like Hitler and Stalin, he encouraged a cult of personality by ensuring that portraits, posters and statues glorifying his rule dominated many public places. He twice led his country into ruinous wars. The first war, with Iran (1980–1988) took place because Saddam feared that the Ayatollah's religious politics would spread to Iraq. This war was hugely expensive and ended in stalemate.

To pay for it, Saddam invaded Iraq's oil-rich neighbour Kuwait, sparking off the Gulf War (1990–1991). International involvement, principally by the USA, drove his army back into Iraq. Saddam's alleged support for international terrorist organisations and supposed possession of weapons of mass destruction led to an invasion by US and allied troops in 2003. Saddam's army was swiftly defeated in battle, but the occupation of the country by Western forces continues to provoke determined resistance. Saddam himself was captured at the end of 2003.

Resisting dictatorship

Some countries have resisted the seemingly inevitable drift towards dictatorship. During the 1990s, following the collapse of communism, the former country of Yugoslavia fractured into smaller states. One of these, Serbia, had been the wealthiest part of Yugoslavia. Its president from 1989, Slobodan Milosevic, instigated a policy of 'ethnic cleansing' to increase Serbia's territory and drive non-Serbs away. Essentially, this policy involved the persecution, rape, and massacre of Croatian, Bosnian and Albanian people living in Yugoslavia. President Milosevic rigged elections to stay in power, and used bribery and violence to strengthen his political position and make money for himself and his family. Eventually, in an election of 2000, Milosevic was defeated by an alliance of eighteen opposition parties. The alliance claimed victory, but Milosevic refused to stand down until an uprising against him forced him from office.

Victims of the war in former Yugoslavia during the 1990s. These Muslim and Croat prisoners are being held by Serbian soldiers. The Serb leader, Slobodan Milosevic, used vote-rigging, bribery and murder to hold on to power.

CHAPTER 6

The Future of Dictatorship

Is dictatorship a style of leadership that is waning in popularity? The signs are that it is, simply because there are fewer dictators in the world today than there were fifty years ago. But even today the most evil dictators in history, such as Stalin and Hitler, continue to enjoy some admiration and support. Clearly the idea of the tyrant or strong leader who can save a nation during times of crisis still has a powerful appeal.

Would-be Russian dictator Vladimir Zhirinovsky, at a rally in the 1990s.

" I say quite plainly, when I come to power there will be a dictatorship. Russia needs a dictatorship now. I will be ruthless. I will close down the newspapers one after the other. I may have to shoot 100,000 people, but the other 300 million will live peacefully. You want to call it Russian fascism – fine. "

Vladimir Zhirinovsky, leader of the Liberal-Democratic Party of Russia, speaking in 1991.

History shows that extreme situations breed extreme politicians. When the Soviet Union's communist regime collapsed, Vladimir Zhirinovsky and his so-called Liberal-Democratic Party of Russia thrived in the lawless atmosphere of the 1990s. Although Zhirinovsky denied that his party was fascist, his utterances and policies clearly bore the hallmarks of extremism. In 1993, Zhirinovsky won 23 per cent of the presidential election vote, although by the year 2000 this support had fallen to 3 per cent. Even after eighty years of brutal totalitarianism, nearly a quarter of all Russians who voted were prepared to support a dictatorial candidate.

In 2004, Russia's president Vladimir Putin won a second term in office. He was elected by 71 per cent of the vote out of the 64 per cent of the total population who turned out to vote. Even assuming that the vote was fairly counted (which is disputed), political opponents and observers felt that Putin's victory was suspect. How could an election be fair, they reasoned, when all of Russia's state controlled television channels supported the president and gave virtually no coverage of other candidates? Time will tell whether Putin, or any other Russian leader, will steer their country back to a dictatorship. With Russia in economic difficulties, with organised crime a fact of daily life, and with many ordinary people nostalgic for the plain but useful government services of the communist era, such a move might be both inevitable and welcomed by much of the population.

Just as communications technology offered the great dictators of the twentieth century unprecedented control over their people, so more advanced forms of communication today may offer a safeguard against dictatorship. The global availability of mobile phones, the Internet and satellite television networks offers citizens of repressive regimes hitherto undreamed of access to alternative sources of information. Even in China, now the world's most powerful communist state, there is a general acceptance that economic success requires a degree of personal freedom. And such freedom is incompatible with the demands of an authoritarian or totalitarian dictatorship.

> ❝❝ **If you want a picture of the future, imagine a boot stamping on a human face – for ever.** ❞❞

The twentieth-century novelist and journalist George Orwell included these words in his most famous novel, 1984, written just after the Second World War. In the book, Orwell imagines a bleak future in which the world is controlled by three rival totalitarian governments, and the crushing effect this has on the human spirit.

> ❝❝ **Nature has left this tincture in the blood, that all men would be tyrants if they could.** ❞❞

The eighteenth-century novelist and journalist Daniel Defoe saw dictatorship as a natural but base human instinct, like greed or lust, which had to be resisted.

Dictator or national hero? Apparently popular with his people, the Cuban communist leader Fidel Castro, seen here in 2001, has run the country for more than forty years.

Timeline

510–27 BCE	Dictators are occasionally chosen to rule in the Roman Republic
1810s–1820s	Wars of independence in Latin America drive away colonial powers of Spain and Portugal, but leave continent open to two centuries of dictatorship
1825	Símon Bolívar becomes dictator of Gran Columbia; his strong, authoritarian rule is unpopular, and he resigns in 1830
1835	Juan Manuel de Rosas seizes power in Argentina; he is overthrown in 1853
1862–1870	Francisco Solano López becomes dictator of Paraguay, and involves his country in a disastrous war with Brazil, Uruguay and Argentina
1922	Benito Mussolini, the first fascist dictator, seizes power in Italy. He joins forces with Nazi Germany during the Second World War. Deposed in 1943, he is executed in 1945.
1923	Mustafa Kemal Ataturk becomes dictator of Turkey and modernises his country. He dies, still in power, in 1938.
1926	Josef Pilsudski leads a *coup* in Poland, and becomes dictator until his death in 1935
1928	Joseph Stalin establishes himself as the sole leader of the Soviet Union, and stays in power until his death in 1953. His policies of enforced collectivisation, and murderous purges, lead to the deaths of millions of Soviet citizens.
1932	Antonio de Oliviera Salazar takes control of Portugal until he is incapacitated by a stroke in 1968
1933	Nazi dictator Adolf Hitler is democratically elected as German Chancellor. Once in power, he bans all opposition and sets Germany on a course for the Second World War. Along with Stalin, Hitler is regarded as one of the most infamous dictators in history.
1939	Following civil war in Spain, General Francisco Franco becomes fascist dictator. He holds on to power until his death in 1975.
1939–1945	The Second World War sees two of the world's greatest dictators, Hitler and Stalin, battle for supremacy. More than fifty million people die during the war.
1942	Hitler's Nazis begin the 'Final Solution' – the extermination of Europe's Jewish population
1945–1948	The Soviet Union oversees the establishment of communist dictatorships loyal to itself in the occupied countries of Eastern Europe
1945–1965	During a period of decolonisation, during which European powers give up their empires, many dictatorships arise in Africa and Asia
1959	Fidel Castro overthrows the corrupt pro-US dictatorship of Fulgencio Batista. Despite invasion and assassination attempts, Castro is still in power in 2004.

1960–1971	East German dictator Walter Ulbricht presides over the building of the Berlin Wall, to stop citizens of his country escaping
1969	Muammar al-Qaddafi seizes power in Libya and establishes an Islamic dictatorship
1971	Ugandan army officer Idi Amin takes power in a *coup*, and establishes a military dictatorship. He seizes privately owned businesses, expels Uganda's Asian population, and murders political opponents. He is deposed in 1979 and flees to Libya.
1971–1989	East German dictator Erich Honecker rules over a country where one in ten people is thought by the authorities to be a police spy
1972	Philippino president Ferdinand Marcos suspends his country's constitution and rules as a dictator, until he is deposed in 1986
1973	The world's first democratically elected Marxist president, Salvador Allende of Chile, is deposed in a US-backed *coup*. He is replaced by the military dictator General Augusto Pinochet.
1977	Dictator Jean Bedel Bokassa, of the Central African Republic, declares himself emperor. He is deposed within two years.
1979	Following the overthrow of the Shah of Iran, religious leader Ayatollah Khomeini returns from exile and sets up an Iranian Islamic republic
1980	Democratically elected President Robert Mugabe comes to power in newly independent Zimbabwe. During the next twenty years he strengthens his power by making opposition to his rule increasingly dangerous.
1988	General Pinochet of Chile is voted out of power and his candidacy for president is rejected beyond 1990
1989	The end of the Cold War sees the fall of all of Eastern Europe's communist dictators. Some, such as East Germany's Erich Honecker, quietly retire. Others, such as Romania's Nicolae Ceauçescu, attempt to massacre protesters, and are in turn executed.
	Serbian president Slobodan Milosevic comes to power, and uses rigged elections, bribery and violence to ensure he remains in control. In 2000, despite losing an election against a coalition of eighteen opposition parties, Milosevic refuses to stand down. An uprising later in that year forces him from office.
1994	The Taliban – a new extreme Islamic fundamentalist regime – emerges in Afghanistan. The intervention of the USA in 2002, following the World Trade Centre terrorist attacks on 11 September 2001, drives the regime from power.
2003	After a twenty-four-year rule, Iraqi dictator Saddam Hussein is deposed by a US-led invasion of his country. The US set up a military administration and subsequently install an interim Iraqi government to govern the country until democratic elections can be held.

Glossary

absolute monarchs kings or queens who rule without any control or restriction over their power

absolute power power without control or restriction

agrarian relating to the countryside and farming

Allies, the during the Second World War, the Allied powers (Britain, France, the USA, the Soviet Union, Canada and Australia) fought against the Axis powers (Germany, Italy and Japan)

authoritarian referring to a regime or society where strict obedience to authority is expected

blocs groups of countries which all share a similar political system

capitalism an economic system in which factories and other businesses and property are owned by individuals, rather than the state

charismatic a personal quality in someone that makes other people admire or follow him or her

Cold War the period after the Second World War, between 1945 and 1991, when the Soviet Union and its allies, and the USA and its allies, were very hostile and mistrustful of each other

collective farms farms in a communist state that are controlled by the government, rather than a landowner

colony a country controlled by another country

communism a political system whereby the state controls the wealth and industry of a country on behalf of its people

Communist Party a political party which believes in the communist philosophy of ruling a country

concentration camp a prison camp for political prisoners, where conditions are usually very brutal

conservative generally speaking, a person or political party in favour of gradual (rather than rapid) change in the governing of a country

coup an armed uprising, usually by the military, against its own government

democratic describes a political system in which the government and law-makers are elected by all of the people

élite the richest and most powerful people in a society

fascist broadly speaking, a follower of a political party which is very right-wing, has one undisputed dictatorial leader, and which advocates extreme, often violent, policies. Fascists usually stress the importance of race and nationhood over that of the individual.

forced labour camps prisons where inmates are forced to work on government approved building projects

fundamentalism an interpretation of religion, usually Muslim or Christian, which advocates extremely strict adherence to that religious belief

ghetto an area of a city in which a particular group of people live

Great Depression a period of worldwide economic slump from 1929 and throughout the 1930s

junta a small group of military commanders who rule a nation following a *coup*

left-wing broadly speaking, favouring socialist policies whereby the state controls industry and wealth on behalf of the people

monarchical relating to a monarchy (rule by a king or queen)

Nazi Party an extreme right-wing political party in power in Germany between 1933 and 1945, which favoured the extermination of Europe's Jews and the establishment of a German empire in the east of Europe and Russia

partisans soldiers who fight behind the lines of an invading country's army

political prisoner a person imprisoned for his or her political beliefs

propaganda biased information given out by a government to make people think in a certain way

Provisional Government a temporary government which takes office until an official, elected government can be set up

referendum a vote on a particular, single issue rather than for a political party

regime another word for a government, usually implying authoritarian or totalitarian overtones

Renaissance a period of European history marking the end of the Middle Ages, when art and science flourished

revolution a dramatic and often violent change in society, or more specifically, in government

right-wing broadly speaking, someone or something which has conservative or fascist political views

shariah (holy) law a legal system based on the teachings of the Koran

social engineering government manipulation of a population in order to produce changes in attitudes or behaviour

Soviet Union a collection of states, centred around the former Russian Empire, controlled by the communist government of Russia

superpowers usually referring to the USA and Soviet Union, the two most powerful nations in the world during the Cold War period

totalitarian relating to a single-party system of government that dominates every aspect of the lives of its citizens

trade union an organisation of workers who join together to try to bring about better pay and conditions for their members

Further Information

Books

Peter Chrisp, *20th Century Leaders – Stalin* (Hodder Wayland, 2002)

David Downing, *Benito Mussolini* (Heinemann, 2001)

David Downing, *Fascism* (Heinemann, 2002)

Paul Dowswell, *20th Century Leaders – Hitler* (Hodder Wayland, 2002)

Nigel Kelly, *Russia and the USSR 1905–1956* (Heinemann, 1997)

Richard Tames, *Dictatorship* (Heinemann, 2002)

George Orwell, *Animal Farm* (Penguin, 1951/first published 1945)

George Orwell, *1984* (Penguin, 2000/first published 1949)

Websites

http://www.thedictatorship.com/
This fascinating website takes an irreverent look at the concept of dictators and dictatorship.

http://en.wikipedia.org/wiki/dictatorship
This website offers a general overview of the topic.

http://www.sparknotes.com/history/
This website offers key information on many of the topics covered in this book, such as Hitler and the Nazis, Stalin and the Soviet Union and Mussolini and Fascist Italy.

http://www.guardian.co.uk/
This website provides recent news reports on dictators and authoritarian or totalitarian regimes.

http://www.nytimes.com/
This website provides recent news reports on dictators and authoritarian or totalitarian regimes, from a US perspective.

Index

Numbers in **bold** refer to illustrations.